A Private War

BOOKS BY ROBERT LAXALT

The Violent Land: Tales the Old Timers Tell

Sweet Promised Land

A Man in the Wheatfield

Nevada

In a Hundred Graves: A Basque Portrait

Nevada: A Bicentennial History

A Cup of Tea in Pamplona

The Basque Hotel

*A Time We Knew: Images of Yesterday in the
Basque Homeland*

Child of the Holy Ghost

A Lean Year and Other Stories

The Governor's Mansion

Dust Devils

*A Private War: An American Code Officer in
the Belgian Congo*

A PRIVATE WAR

An American Code Officer in the Belgian Congo

Robert Laxalt

UNIVERSITY OF NEVADA PRESS / RENO & LAS VEGAS

University of Nevada Press, Reno, Nevada 89557 USA

Copyright © 1998 by Robert Laxalt

Manufactured in the United States of America

Design by Carrie Nelson House

Library of Congress Cataloging-in-Publication Data

Laxalt, Robert, 1923–

A private war : an American code officer in the Belgian
Congo / Robert Laxalt.

p.   cm.

ISBN 0-87417-323-X (alk. paper). —

ISBN 0-87417-324-8 (pbk. : alk. paper)

1. Laxalt, Robert, 1923– . 2. World War, 1939–1945—
Secret service—United States. 3. World War, 1939–
1945—Cryptography. 4. World War, 1939–1945—Congo
(Democratic Republic)—Kinshasa. 5. World War,
1939–1945—Personal narratives, American. 6. Uranium
mines and mining—Congo (Democratic Republic)—
History—20th century. 7. World War, 1939–1945—
Equipment and supplies. 8. Cryptographers—United
States—Biography. I. Title.

D810.S8L395 1998   98-11581

940.54'8673—dc21   CIP

The paper used in this book meets the requirements of
American National Standard for Information Sci-
ences—Permanence of Paper for Printed Library Materials, ANSI Z39.48-1984. Binding materials were se-
lected for strength and durability.

Frontispiece: Robert Laxalt, shortly after his return from
the Congo. Courtesy, Robert Laxalt.

First Printing

07 06 05 04 03 02 01 00 99 98   5 4 3 2 1

for Joyce

again and always

This book, or more precisely *memoir*, had a curious genesis.

My son and I had gone to my father's old sheep camp in the Sierra. One night around the campfire, the conversation turned to war and "a man's duty to serve his country." Even as I uttered it, that phrase sounded almost embarrassing in its old-fashioned quality. The debacle that Viet Nam turned into had gone a long way toward destroying the credibility of war and patriotism with which my generation had grown up.

Our talk went back to World War II, the war in which I had grown up. That war was probably the last one where words like *my country, patriotism, duty,* and *service* would flame white hot.

My son knew that I had gone to Africa in that war, but not as a member of the armed forces. He did not know why I, being exempt, even went. I tried to explain my own and my generation's attitude toward service to one's country. Again, the words I used seemed outdated and downright corny.

He was mystified at my fury at not being allowed to carry a gun into battle, my humiliation at being rejected by the armed forces because of a childhood heart murmur, and my desperate desire to go *overseas*.

Since I am a writer who has written considerably about my youth, he asked why I hadn't written about this experience. I told him that it was still too painful for me to close with and that I wasn't the kind of writer who laments about his misunderstood youth. We let the conversation end there.

As time passed, I wondered about my decision. Finally, I unearthed the journal I had kept during that time. I had never shown it to anyone. Some of it was childish and self-conscious, but there was enough there that had the validity to write about.

A Private War

In the last year of World War II, in spite of my country's efforts to thwart me, I sort of went to war.

This is a record of that time, drawn from a journal I more or less kept, entries expanded upon and memories they triggered.

Somewhere on the Atlantic Seaboard

The convoy was spread out upon the sea in the shape of an immense fan, waiting to close ranks and join the ordered form it would keep in its passage across the Atlantic. Gray ships upon a gray sea under a gray sky. Liberty ships that rolled and lumbered awkwardly, laden with troops and supplies for the European theater of war.

The convoy was flanked by long, narrow destroyer escorts that darted nervously about, cleaving the water as cleanly as a knife. Curling white wakes washed back from their prows. They in turn were flanked by destroyers that lay farther out, so that their shapes were indistinct in the gray day. They moved all in a line, ominous and constrained as though holding back their deadly capacity for destruction. They were not unlike wolves guarding their pups.

I had come up from below decks, as the sailors called it in a jargon that was new to me. Someone had said there were over a hundred ships in the convoy sailing out of Virginia. I could believe it. Standing by the rail, I tried to count them, then gave up the job because the ships that led the convoy were already disappearing from view over the distant horizon.

A few hours before, I had followed the single file of soldiers with steel helmets and full packs, but no rifles, climbing the gangway to the looming gray hulk that was my own particular Liberty ship. Only a few days before that, at Camp Patrick Henry in Virginia, I had been issued two sets of the khaki uniforms that I had dreamed of wearing for so long. They were without insignia or rank, but I didn't care, because they were khaki and they were military uniforms.

A full pack of C rations had been issued to me, along with sulfa, a brown woolen blanket, and a square of canvas that was called a shelter half. I accepted these with equanimity, but when a steel helmet and a gas mask were handed to me, I felt faintly ridiculous.

Climbing the steps of the gangway, a bulky tough-talking soldier in front of me turned and said out of the corner of his mouth, "Crack invasion troops. That's what we are."

That remark mystified me, and I wondered who in hell we were supposed to invade. *I* knew I was going to Africa, but the war was done there. The

Germans had been driven north, and Africa was in Allied hands.

I suppressed the temptation to tell the soldier where the convoy was going.

Already, I had gotten used to keeping that secret. Because they had been delivered in such stern terms, I remembered vividly my instructions not to reveal where I was going, and in even more severe terms, what my duties were to be when we got there. I was mildly thankful that someone at the State Department had taken the precaution of telling me my destination and that my duties there were very important. I would probably have volunteered all that in my first conversation with a German spy. I was becoming aware that candor was not always a virtue.

The tough-talking soldier had probably not even been told what his destination was, though he should have guessed it pretty closely, since none of the troops were armed. Later, I was to learn that the soldier's brother had won the Congressional Medal of Honor somewhere in the Pacific, and had died for it there. The soldier had known all along that he wouldn't be sent to another war theater. Because he wanted to believe it and was jealous of his dead brother, he had simply made up his mind that he was a combat soldier and his comrades crack invasion troops.

The cabin to which I was assigned had turned

out to be a small, airless enclosure with tiers of bunks on two sides. Six men in a cubbyhole, and officers at that. I had thrown my pack on a bunk and gone up to the deck, ignoring the questions my cabin mates threw at me.

My ship had been positioned near the end of the convoy. The first time I went to find my cabin, it was on weaving, unsteady legs that had never been confronted with a rolling deck. From the fantail, I had an unobstructed view of the receding shore-line of the United States. Here and there along the rail, small groups of soldiers stood, gazing longingly at the vanishing shore. "Good-bye, good old U.S.A.," one of them said. The others seemed to find it impossible to speak through the constrictions in their throats. Others muttered single-word assents and sounds.

I raised my eyes from the white wake below me, frothing and filling with shapes that resembled octopus eyes, and looked at the land that had rejected me. "God damn you. I hope I never see you again."

University of Santa Clara, California

I was standing at ease on the turfed ROTC drill ground, chest heaving from the calisthenics the corps was being put through by the upper-class cadet commander. The autumn sun of California shone down on the drill ground, but the air was golden from leaves losing their summer green. The cadet commander had given us permission to take off our shirts. Torsos tanned by summer were streaming with sweat.

In normal times, calisthenics had been a haphazard effort listlessly ordered and grudgingly performed. Military classes had been a farce where instructors gave examination questions they knew nobody would study for, except those who were seriously aiming for a commission. It was tradition that student cadets prepared themselves for unanswerable questions by carrying crib notes into class.

The cadets did not even bother to conceal their cribs, openly leaving them beside their examination blue books. Long ago, the military department had reconciled itself to the vain hope that at least something of value would wash off on the cadets from the mere effort of preparing crib notes.

But then Pearl Harbor had happened, and things got serious. It did not come in a hurry. Not much had changed through the spring semester after December 7 except a slowly dawning realization that the country was at war and the war might even filter onto the cloistered campus.

By the time summer had ended and the autumn semester began, the deed had been accomplished. At the University of Santa Clara, a small male Jesuit campus that did not contain even five hundred students, nearly every face was a familiar face.

And now, some of the faces I expected to see in the fall were gone to war as volunteers.

The alternative of getting into the reserve and thereby postponing the draft had sent students scurrying to reserve recruiting offices or, of all things, taking ROTC seriously.

Everyone was resigned to the inevitability of service somewhere—Army, Navy, Marines. That was not the issue. The issue now was to postpone service as long as possible. There were no heroes on this ROTC drill ground.

My curiosity was aroused by the aspect of a cadet officer hurrying across the drill ground. This was an oddity in itself. In my memory, nobody had ever hurried across the drill ground. The proper pace was dragging feet and a slouching posture.

The hurrying cadet snapped to attention before the cadet commander and actually saluted. He did not seem to be affected by the low moan emanating from the cadet ranks. In what I supposed was proper military demeanor, the cadet handed the cadet commander a message. The commander scrutinized it with proper gravity.

"Private Robert Laxalt! Fall out!"

Revealing that he had never given the order before, the cadet commander repeated his command twice more.

"He's got to be kidding," I said and was rewarded by a remark from one of my comrades, "The C.O. has lost his mind."

Still, there was something in the cadet commander's voice that said he was not kidding. Dutifully, I made my way to the cadet commander and the courier who had brought the message. I came to attention, but I absolutely could not bring myself to salute.

"Yeah?" I said.

"The proper response to a summons from the C.O. is 'Yes, sir'."

I decided against tempting fate. "Yes, sir."

"I know this is going to hurt you," the cadet commander said with broad sarcasm in his voice, "but you are dismissed from the troop."

"What's up?"

"You flunked the physical. You've got a heart murmur."

"Oh, that. I've had that since I was a kid," I said. "Rheumatic fever. Pay no attention to it. It's nothing."

"It's enough to keep you out of the service."

In keeping with the mood of the ROTC troop, I was tempted to laugh. It was the first time I was faced with the realization that I might be sitting out the war, safe at home in Carson City while my friends were in the service. The prospect of going back home was suddenly unattractive.

Carson City, Nevada

In the days before the war, nothing much distinguished my home town of Carson City from a thousand other small towns scattered across the United States.

Generations came and went, children were born, the old died, summers were hot and languid. In those times, the young of Carson City searched for shade, hiking up King's Canyon along a creek fed by winter storms until we reached the waterfall. We crouched at its base and were rapt with the roar of running waters and the cooling spray of water from melting snows, and once in a while we caught a trout with fishing poles we had whittled out of willow branches. I was to remember that cooling spray and lulling peace more than a few times in the suffocating jungle of Equatorial Africa.

Autumn and school began at the same time, and the first yellow leaves appeared in the tops of the cottonwood trees.

Winter came and went with the magic of first snow and the excitement of streaking down steep streets on homemade skis.

Then the war came, and all of that was ended.

Carson City, Nevada

The war caught the town unawares. Except for the college-bound, most grown men had never been out of sight of Carson City.

A trip to Reno thirty miles away was an adventure, and a trip to San Francisco in neighboring California was almost unheard of. Carson City's males suddenly found themselves scattered around the globe.

The draft was the single phenomenon that propelled my generation and the one before it to alien settings.

The word *draft* was a word whose inevitability allowed for no alternative. For married men, it meant separation from family and friends. For those who yearned for heroics, it was the passport to adventure, glory, and honor.

But the honor I secretly yearned for was to be denied me. When I was six years old, I was stricken with rheumatic fever, and it left me with a heart murmur that was to label me unfit for military service. That I was an athlete of varsity rank meant nothing. I was declared unfit, and the damage was done to my pride. The Selective Service System might as well have denounced me as subhuman.

San Francisco, California

Sorry, young man. This war you sit out.

FEBRUARY, 1944

San Francisco, California

I appreciate how much you want to be a combat flier, but I can't pass you with a heart like that.

FEBRUARY, 1944

San Francisco, California

The Marines pride themselves on being tough. We've got our standards. They don't include accepting bum hearts.

FEBRUARY, 1944

San Francisco, California

Your heart muscle is strong. That's from sports. But you have a leaky valve in there somewhere. I just can't pass you.

Air Force. Marines. Navy. Army. The answer was al-
ways the same—physically unfit for military service.
With each rejection, another door closed.

———❖———

MARCH, 1944

Carson City, Nevada

Our son has to risk his life going to war while you
stay home all safe and sound. Something stinks
here.

MARCH, 1944

Carson City, Nevada

I didn't know they served 4F's in here. We'll do our
drinking somewhere else.

MARCH, 1944

Carson City, Nevada

Football star. Basketball. Boxer. But not strong
enough to go to war. Smells like draft-dodger to
me.

The taunts and contempt were, if anything, worse than formal rejection. There was no choice but to get out of town, out of Nevada.

⟫●⟪

MARCH, 1944

Carson City, Nevada

U.S. Senator Patrick McCarran
Senate Office Building
Washington, D.C.

Dear Senator McCarran:

I want to serve my country, but the armed forces won't let me. I have tried to enlist in the Air Force, Marines, Navy, and Army. Because of a heart murmur incurred when I was a child, I have been declared unfit for military service.

On the advice of your political friends in Carson City, the capital of Nevada, I am appealing to you to place me in the State Department in Washington, D.C.

I would like to serve overseas, preferably in a dangerous post, so that I can feel I am helping my country in time of war. Though you know my father, who is a Nevada sheepman, I am attaching my background.

Respectfully,
Robert Laxalt

Off the Atlantic Shore

They must have been talking about me while I was on deck. I could sense that from the way the conversation abruptly ended when I stood framed in the doorway. Purposefully, my glance swept the cabin. The cramping in my stomach eased. Their appraisal of me was not unfriendly except from one man with Teutonic blue eyes. Some of them looked sheepish, like little boys caught out. An older, lanky officer with a Texas drawl and captain's bars on his shirt regarded me with furrowed brows and an openly quizzical expression.

From our first brush when we had come on board, I remembered his name—Tom Conrad. I also remembered the name of the antagonistic man with the hot, blue eyes. His name was Heine.

Since they were soldiers and officers, I should have suspected the first thing they would do when their men had been seen to would be to make up their bunks and put their things away neatly. One wall of the cabin contained six little cabinets with bracing slats against the rolling of the ship. Five of the cabinets were filled. Now, my cabin mates were sitting or sprawling on their bunks throwing the bull until dinner call would be sounded.

There was a murmured greeting from some of them as I made my way to my bunk. I acknowledged it with a curt nod of my chin. Over the last two years of my private hell, I had developed a closed-in mask of a face with narrowed eyes that I like to think glinted with faint hostility and lips that were twisted in faint disdain. My nose, almost aquiline, was flattened out a little at the bridge, where it had been broken in an amateur boxing match, and thin white scars slicing through my eyebrows added to the effect I wanted to create. It was my protection against the world. Only I knew how fragile that façade was, how easily it could break down under scrutiny.

Back in the cabin, I dug into the duffel bag that had been issued to me, taking out only my shaving tools and hair tonic. I pulled the strings of the duffel bag shut extra tightly. Stuffed into the bottom of the bag, under my extra khaki uniform, was everything I wanted to hide—a civilian suit, shirts, stockings and underwear and a pair of civilian dress shoes. Putting the toilet articles away in the last remaining cabinet, I made up my bunk.

"Mac, where in what man's army did you learn to make up a bunk?"

The voice was a Texas drawl, and I knew immediately whose it was. The first arrow of exposure fixed me in frozen posture. I felt Tom Conrad's big hands clasp me around my upper arms and move me gently but firmly away. Then he made up my bunk so that the woolen blanket was stretched taut as a sail in the wind. Conrad leaned back with his hands on his hips. "Now you pass muster," he drawled good naturedly, and I was disarmed. I sat down on my bunk and lighted a cigarette with fingers that trembled only slightly. I was in the presence of demigods, Atlantian figures not only in uniform but with shining officer's bars, campaign ribbons, and at least one Purple Heart.

"Where you from, son?" Conrad drawled in a fatherly tone, even though he and I couldn't have been separated by ten years.

"Nevada."

The single word must have conjured up images. "I'll be damned," Tom Conrad said. "I've never met anybody from Nevada before."

"Remind me never to play craps with you." That came from another officer whose name I remembered was Higgins.

Shaking my head, I said, "That's not so. I don't even know how to play craps. That's for tourists."

The banter about Nevada and gambling and legal whores got warmer, and I felt my tension grow loose. I grinned at them when they made me confess I had gone to legal whorehouses. I was just beginning to say to myself, "It's just like I wanted it to be: comrades gone to war. I'm free at last." Then I was jerked back to reality.

"What's your outfit?" the man called Heine said in a cold voice.

"Lay off, Heinie," the poker player called Higgins said.

"What d'you mean, 'lay off.' It's the question all of you were asking."

I felt the eyes of the room swiveling toward me. "None," I said, hearing the hoarseness in my voice.

"What does that mean, 'None'?" asked Heine.

"Just what it's supposed to mean. I'm by myself."

"That doesn't make sense," Heine said. "What's your rank?"

"I don't have a rank," I said. "Oh," I said, remembering. "I'm a casual officer, I guess."

"Well, what do you do?"

"I'm not supposed to say."

"What kind of bullshit is that?" Heine was openly hostile now. "If you're in the Army, you got to have a rank and you got to have a reason for being here."

"I've got a reason," I started to say, but Tom Conrad cut me short. "Stow it, Heine," he said in hard tones. "What the man does and who he belongs to is none of our business. If he's government, that's all you have to know." He turned to me with sudden doubt showing. "You *are* government?"

This time, I was convincing. "I'm government," I said. "State Department. But I can't tell you anything more."

"How in hades did you work that?" said Higgins wonderingly.

"Through my senator. I couldn't get in the Army."

"You're 4F?" Higgins was incredulous.

I could not bring myself to acknowledge the hated word. I stared at Higgins shamefaced.

"Beautiful," Higgins said. "I tried for two years to get 4F. The bastards caught me anyway."

"But if you're 4F," Tom Conrad said with sincere puzzlement, "what in hell are you doing out here on a troopship with a German U-boat ready to torpedo your ass off?"

There was no way I could make them understand. "I asked for it."

"You're mad, Mac," Higgins said. "Stark raving mad."

"Or else he's a Jew." It was Heine again. "Jews always come out on the easy end."

"Not that I give a damn," Higgins said to me, "but are you a Jew?"

"I'm Basque." I was instantly sorry that I had said the word.

"Basque," Higgins said. "What's that?"

"I'm not quite sure," I said. "I've never have been able to get it straight. My folks come from somewhere between France and Spain."

"Or Palestine?" Heine broke in. "You a Jew-lover?"

It was Washington, D.C., where I'd gotten my first inkling that Jews and Negroes were not supposed to be liked. The revelation had genuinely puzzled me. I told Conrad, "I don't think I know any Jews."

"Man, you are incredible," said Tom Conrad. "I don't suppose you know any niggers, either."

I was disappointed in Tom Conrad. "Well, there was an old man named Andy who was the shoe-shine boy at the barber shop," I said to Tom. "But nobody made anything out of it. He was just a quiet old man. And once there were two Negro kids who went to school in Carson. George and Lonnie were their names. We were good friends, but they went away in a year."

"You'll get a chance to know a lot more of them pretty soon," Tom Conrad said enigmatically. "Then you can find out whether you like darkies or not."

I caught myself on the brink of nodding my head. I guessed that at least Conrad knew where we were going, probably because he was the top-rank-ing officer on board. I just looked at him with a poker face.

"Good man," he said, reading through my silence and approving.

Dinner call sounded, and they swung off their bunks. As for me, I decided to stay where I was. Their voices faded, but not enough to keep me from hearing Heine say loudly, "Fucking New York Jew draft-dodging 4F sonofabitch."

"He's from Nevada," said Higgins with sarcasm. "By all means, don't drop that from his sins."

"Heine! Shut your mouth," said Tom Conrad. "That's an order."

Snatches of words drifted back to me. "Better not crowd that guy . . . broken nose . . . scars . . . he might give you a big surprise."

I lit a cigarette in the silent cabin. My hand was shaking so badly that I couldn't make contact between the match and the end of the cigarette. I let the match drop to the floor and splutter out. *It's beginning all over again,* I cried to myself. *I thought it would end when I left that damned country. But it's not going to.*

After a while, I stood up in sudden decision. I gathered up my shaving tools and stuffed them back into the duffel bag. Stripping the blanket and shelter half off my bunk, I rolled them roughly into a bundle and headed out the door.

The deck was deserted and dark because of the blackout against submarines. Sooner or later, the U-boats would begin stalking the convoy. The sky had cleared, and the stars shone brightly in the wall of night above. Teetering uncertainly on the rolling deck, I tried to make out the stacks of life rafts I had seen during the day. When I found one stack that seemed out of sight of the bridge, I heaved my pack and blankets over the top and climbed in after them.

The life rafts were oval in shape, and their slatted bottoms were long enough for me to lie down on. For more depth, I used my trench knife to cut through the rough ropes that bound the slats to the tubular sides of the life raft. I was rendering the upper rafts useless, but I really couldn't believe there were submarines lurking in the black depths outside the perimeter of the convoy.

The canvas shelter half was only big enough to cover part of my cave. I lashed it to the tubular sides with the fragments of rope left dangling when I had cut them through. Using my life jacket as a pillow, I laid my lone blanket under it with everything on it but my combat boots. Through the aperture above, I could see the stars in the sky. Except for the roll of the ship and the tang of brine in the air, I could have been in my father's mountain sheep camp. *That part of America I will miss,* I thought. *That and my family, but nothing else.* For a moment I felt free, and then I remembered the officer's cabin I had abandoned. "I can't. I won't go through it again."

Somewhere in mid-Atlantic

"Let's talk."

I dutifully followed Tom Conrad to the ship's rail. We stood together, looking down at the white wash of the ship's progress through the sea. Not too far distant, the lethal profile of a destroyer escort kept pace.

"I feel safer with those babies riding herd on the convoy," I said. "Any sign of U-boats yet, Captain?"

Tom Conrad shook his head, "Dusk is the time they choose to make their presence known," he said. "When the convoy is in profile. *Submarine time,* the sailors call it. Keep it to yourself, but our afterdeck is on alert to arm their depth charges."

I followed the captain's gaze to the afterdeck and a flurry of activity going on there. Two huge mechanical devices that resembled catapults had been stripped of their covering and were being armed with what seemed to be outsized oil barrels.

"Depth charges," said Tom Conrad. "Looks like we're in for some fireworks tonight. But we won't be watching."

"Why not?"

"We'll be below decks until the 'all clear' is sounded," said Conrad. "I've okayed a fight night to keep the men occupied." He paused meaningfully. "That's where you come in."

"Meaning what?"

"Meaning you're being set up for the main event."

"Heine?"

"Yep. Him and his Hialeah buddies are the big promoters."

"What if I say 'no way'?"

"They'll make life unpretty for you. You've gotten a taste of it—Jew boy and draft-dodger."

"I'm Basque and not a fighter. I'm a lover."

"It won't wash. Your fight scars and busted nose show you're no stranger to boxing. I'm right, ain't I?" he drawled.

"Okay," I said. "So I've had a few go-rounds in the ring. Strictly amateur. I'm not taking on any pro. There's a difference, you know. I took on a pro once. I was lucky to come out alive."

"Batalucco's no pro," said Conrad. "But he's good. Chicago Golden Gloves champion."

"He's good, all right," I said. "I saw him go the other night. He's a heavy hitter." I stared out to sea.

"If you don't want to go, I'll cover for you. Orders from the ranking officer on board. Me."

"I don't need that." Stung, I said, "I'm trying to figure out a way to stick it into Heine and his Hialeah crowd. I'll go if you tell them you had a hell of a time selling me. Put twenty bucks on Batalucco. They'll follow your lead. In hundreds. I want to hurt them bad."

"As far as I'm concerned," said Conrad, "you've never put on gloves before."

The setting was not unlike that of a prizefight smoker. A surround of faces. A swell of voices. Air so thick with smoke that I could hardly breathe. I tried to affect the demeanor of a boxer waiting for the bell to sound, shuffling my feet and flexing my arms. Heine was the second for Batalucco, rubbing Vaseline on his face and massaging his arms. Batalucco shuffled his legs professionally, shadow-boxing with short punches, pausing every once in a while to size me up.

"I'm not fooling him a bit," I thought to myself. "He's smart enough to know I've been around."

The bell sounded, and the time for play-acting was over. I moved to the center of the ring, my left hand positioned for a jab. If my instincts were right, Batalucco with his muscular shoulders was a slugger. We touched gloves and moved apart.

I was right. We had hardly separated when Batalucco started the action with a wild right. Slipping the punch, I pumped a fast left jab into Batalucco's face, drawing first blood. We clinched, and I stole a look at Heine's face at ringside, florid and angry as if he had been cheated.

At round's end, I went back to my corner and a beaming triumphant Conrad. "All right! All right!" Conrad was shouting in my ear. The round had clearly been mine. One down and four to go.

The next two rounds went the way of the first. It was time to start following my jabs with left hooks that left Batalucco's face bloody. The crowd was really shouting now.

I had my fight plan firm in my head. Batalucco was primed, and I was going for a knockout. That way, Batalucco would have nothing to base his "the referee's crazy" complaint on.

Working Batalucco to the center of the ring, I saw my chance and put everything I had into one punch, an overhand right. But the punch never landed. It went sailing over Batalucco's head, taking me with it. The deep roaring in my ears was pierced with shouts and screams, not from pain but fear and panic. The crescendo of sound came first from an ear-splitting explosion and then shouts and screams from every voice in the crowd mixed with the crash of tables and chairs and everything else in the below-decks. I had a mental image of our ship standing on its head. The ship seemed to be intact. It fell back into the sea with a jolt every bit as devastating as the first explosion.

"Torpedo! Torpedo!" a hundred voices were shouting. "We're going down."

Nobody offered a hand to anybody. There was only one gangway out of the below-decks, and everybody was heading for it at the same time. Utter chaos reigned as desperate men swore, pushed and pulled, swung with both hands at the man in front of him to get his place in the jammed gangway.

Heroics were not considered as each man fought for his life. And I was not excluded.

"No torpedo! No torpedo! Depth charge! Depth charge!" from the M.P.s guarding the top of the gangway made no impression at all when the panic began. Then, the blasting of heavy .45 pistols were heard. The noise and the panic began to subside when the M.P.s shouted ominously, "Nobody gets out of the hold! We'll kill you if you try!"

One man tried. He made it as far as the head of the crowd. Without a trace of emotion, one M.P. shot him in the knee. He lay on the stairs clutching his bleeding knee.

So much for the nobility of man, echoed through my consciousness.

An officer with a resounding voice was repeating himself. "It was a depth charge with a short fuse."

There was no reaction to the shooting, probably because sensibilities had died in that confined space called the below-decks.

Casablanca, Africa

I had smelled Africa for the first time the evening before. It was a fecund scent borne by land breezes from deep in the interior. It sent shivers coursing up and down my spine. We had rocked gently in the still waters of the harbor. Only a few lights had come on to show that Casablanca lay almost hidden in the near darkness.

On the gun turret that hovered over the deck, a match had flared, breaking the darkness. It was followed by the crack of a rifle, a metallic clang of a bullet striking metal and the whining echo of a ricochet as the bullet spent itself.

"For Christ's sake, no matches!" a voice of authority had snapped. "Casablanca is loaded with Nazi snipers waiting to pick us off."

This time, the shiver had not been from the discovery that a different continent had its own smell. "Well, the war has finally caught up with me," I thought exultantly.

Now with the first light, the harbor and the white houses at Casablanca began to take shape. The harbor was a graveyard of bombed ships, some dismasted, others capsized, and still others run aground. A segment of the convoy began a weaving approach through the wreckage. Our ship was one of the first to tie up at the docks. It was greeted by a squeaking swarm of Arabs dressed in

27

rags, with their heads wrapped in greasy turbans. None of them looked as if they had ever taken a bath.

One of the ship's crew stepped up to the dock with a knowing expression on his face. He pulled a handful of small coins—nickels and dimes and pennies—out of his pocket. Taking careful aim, he arched the coins over the center of the swarm. That set off a scramble of men hitting and clawing at each other for the coins. It was a nightmarish scramble where cries rose from squeaks to screams.

I was witnessing something I would never have seen in America, I thought with an emotion close to horror—grown men reduced to fighting for coins. I was not ashamed of them. I was ashamed *for* them.

A troop of Senegalese soldiers with statuesque frames and ebony-black skin materialized out of an alley. They were wearing smart khaki uniforms, and they were armed with long batons. They knew what they were about. Without emotion, they marched into the swarm of beggars, and the squeaking turned to screams of pain. The beggars fled into the alleyways of Casablanca.

When the dock was cleared, a visibly shaken Tom Conrad cried out in disgust, "Is that what we came to save?"

Off the coast of Africa

We had followed the shoreline southwards from Casablanca, depositing troops along the Gold Coast and the Ivory Coast with short stays in Accra and Dakar.

Dakar is famous for its whorehouses. I don't suppose there are many brothels that can boast prostitutes of a dozen nationalities—all housed in a rambling white mansion. Before the war, the villa and its gardens had belonged to a rich merchant who had made a lot of money in prostitution before moving on to a higher calling, drugs.

Whether I wanted to see an African brothel was of no importance. The merchant mariners made it an obligatory ritual for their passengers. The last of the soldiers on our ship had been dropped off, and the merchant mariners had taken over the ship. They took me by the hand and led me to what in their eyes was Dakar's leading point of historic interest.

Prostitutes—French, Spanish, Italian, Arabic, Scandinavian, and even German—floated through the villa and its garden. Rivalries and animosities did not seem to exist among the women, and their common trait seemed to be good humor first before leading a guest up the staircase to a elaborately got-up room with an Arabic flavor. Someone had told them I was an American, which seemed to be a rarity. Before I knew it, an Arab whore painted to the gills got into an argument with a fiery Spanish whore as to who would savor me first. In the shouting match, I managed to make my escape.

When our convoy had had its run, I went on by air down the coast of Africa, in little BOAC and Sabena passenger planes, stopping at such places as Pointe Noire and E'byville, bouncing in metal bucket seats. The shoreline between land and sea was uniformly spectacular, the great green jungle divided from the blue Atlantic by a ribbon of blinding white sand. At the juncture where the roiling Congo River emptied into the Atlantic, we turned inland, following the great river along the Equator into darkest Africa.

My companion, Clete, and I had made each other's company in Dakar, the capital of French West Africa. He was an old Africa hand. His work was finding mahogany forests in the bush. His face showed the ravages of bush life and gin. He was dressed in worn twill shorts, bush jacket, and shapeless bush hat.

"I suppose you know what you're getting into," Clete said when I told him my destination was the Belgian Congo.

I shook my head, and he intoned solemnly, "Malaria, dysentery, heat, humidity, jaundice, boils, blacks who will steal you blind, malaria, malaria, ad infinitum. In case they didn't tell you, you'll be straddling the Equator."

The Leopoldville airport was a long, uncertain rectangle cut out of the jungle. The BOAC passenger plane cleared the last tree barrier and dropped onto the airfield, skittering in the direction of the terminal.

"Something's up," said Clete as we disembarked. I followed his gaze to where a knot of blacks and a uniformed Belgian officer were clustered. A black in ragged khaki shorts was kneeling on the ground, and the Belgian officer was standing over him. The Belgian officer was holding what I learned was a *chacot,* a whip with long leather thongs whose ends were tipped with metal.

The whip whistled and the air seemed filled with a bloody haze. Every lash was followed by a scream of agony. When the prescribed number of lashes had been delivered, the black's skin from neck to waist was a mass of blood with ribs shining through.

"What did he do to deserve a beating like that?" I asked Clete when the spectacle was over.

"He stole a pack of cigarettes from a Belgian."

"Good God!"

"You ain't seen nothin' yet," said Clete, reciting a litany of blacks being clubbed off the sidewalk for not stepping aside for a white man, and the common practice of a driver turning back to run his car over a black whom he'd already run over. In the first instance, the death of a black cost the driver nothing if the black died. If he lived, the driver would have to pay indemnity to the black's family.

This I could not accept as truth until I had to code a report on a Belgian troop invading a village where a white missionary had been killed by natives. The penalty was quick and thorough. When it was over, slightly less than one hundred natives had been shot.

"Welcome to the Congo," Clete said when we parted company.

Leopoldville, Belgian Congo, Africa

The American Consulate General that would be my home was located discreetly on a street that historically housed foreign legations. This is customary in the Foreign Service. Proximity gave the legations a chance to spy on each other. It also saved diplomatic invitees the trouble of traveling long distances to attend each other's interminable soirées, where one consulate officer could try to lure another into giving away a secret. Friendliness and laughter with each other was the mood. The soirée on its surface appeared to be a gathering of close friends. Or so it seemed to me in my first months in the Congo.

This was my indoctrination to diplomatic social life, to which I had never been exposed. Having come from a very small town, I was at first bewildered and impressed with it all—formal manners, polite laughter, serious conversations about world politics, evening dress of tropical white gowns and tuxedos, sultry flirtations and arranged rendezvous, violin and string instruments playing in the background, champagne and Irish whiskey, Scotch and Russian vodka. My first impression was that of unflawed social gatherings with an international flavor.

To my surprise, the polished atmosphere was not what it seemed to be. Once having gained a morsel of intelligence, the diplomat would take his bon-homie and hand-kissing leave, go back to his lega-tion office, make out his dispatch, and seal it for his code officer to send out the next day.

If the intelligence was of ordinary interest, the message from the United States legation to an Allied home office elsewhere, or to the State De-partment in Washington, would go out in an ordi-nary code drawn from Brown's Code Book. This discretion seemed a futile exercise to me when I learned that every foreign legation, ally or enemy, possessed a copy of the Brown's Code Book. But of course, I could say nothing in protest. Most of it was *war news*, condensed and censored and al-ready printed in newspapers.

Messages and reports of genuine importance, such as too-frequent meetings between Germans and the Belgian government-in-residence, went out in a confidential code that a legation protected with its life. I know, because it was my function to write out and dispatch all coded messages. For this, I had been trained in the confidential cryp-tography section of the State Department in Washington, D.C., having passed muster as intel-ligent, loyal, and hard-working.

Confidential reports ranged from important to vitally important, as it turned out when uranium entered the picture. This kept my job from ever bridging routinely into the ordinary. Since I took my responsibility seriously, I was irritated when a confidential report was by nature unimportant or waspish. One would be surprised to know how much social information of no value made the confidential rating. Also, how waspish diplomats can be. Still, diplomatic gossip can lighten a code officer's day. But the fact that I was helping the war effort was important enough for me, compared to contributing nothing toward the war. And I had actually achieved my goal of getting *overseas*.

Our American legation was headed up by a consul general, a very proper Ivy League product whose appointment to the Foreign Service had been bolstered by the fact of his family's wealth.

The consul general, whom I will call J. Wesley Hale, did not inquire too deeply into the legation's affairs. He preferred the social whirl, and I got to know him fairly well, since most of the legation's society gossip came from him to me for coding. His contact was the wife of an official of the Belgian government-in-residence. Everybody on Legation Row knew about Hale's torrid affair, but nobody cared. From what I could gather, this kind of relationship was not unusual in the world of diplomacy. At that, Hale's reports sometimes bore important intelligence inadvertently placed in the context of general gossip.

This had mainly to do with the doings of the diplomatic elite. For example, were the British to be trusted in keeping a secret? Were the visiting Germans really businessmen, or spies undercover, as our visitors turned out to be?

In the consul general's frequent absences from his office, a vice-consul actually ran the legation's function. Harry Wolfe was a direct opposite of J. Wesley Hale. He was a Princeton graduate for whom the Foreign Service had long been a calling.

Harry's and my relationship was professional at the beginning because we had to work closely together. He was a tall, rangy man with sandy hair and blue eyes that advertised frankness in diplomatic affairs. He had a penchant for adventure, and so did I.

The economic attaché to the Consulate General, Dan Weathers, was a burly man who was not an Ivy League product, and showed it. He dealt with his counterparts in business and economics in a bullying manner. Since the area of business and economics did not concern my office, I was mercifully spared his company, except on one rare occasion.

Of two secretaries in the office, one was a girl, Joselle, of mixed French and Arab blood. She was multilingual, an invaluable asset to anyone working with a handful of nationalities at the same time. I think she was in love with Harry, but he remained faithful to a fiancée in Spain. The lineup of countries in World War II in Europe had parted them, but they somehow managed to communicate through Tangier, an open city.

The least and last member of the staff was a barefoot young black whose Swahili name was Mbote. Out of curiosity, Mbote had come in from the bush to see Leopoldville. He stumbled into the Consulate General by accident and was immediately employed as an errand boy. Mbote learned some American ways, but he could not rid himself of native habits. Whenever he was asked to go to the post office for stamps, he would return with them at a dog trot, the stamps held to the top of his head by a rock. The system worked. He never lost a stamp.

Finally there was Doc Pogue, a thin man with a balding head and the most piercing eyes I had ever encountered. When I was introduced to him, I felt that he was reading my mind. It was not until later that I remembered Harry said not a word about Doc Pogue's function in the legation or what his background was.

Doc Pogue drifted into the legation only on rare occasion, spent some time with Harry behind closed doors, and nodded to us on his way out.

When I asked Harry who Doc was and what he did, Harry said vaguely that Doc Pogue was attached to the Office of War Information in Leopoldville and that his job was to disseminate American propaganda in the Congo.

Propagandizing a supposedly friendly nation didn't make sense, and I wondered about it.

Something else didn't make sense. There was a constant stream of American visitors to the legation. They all seemed to be cut of the same cloth, quiet men who didn't bother to exchange more than a greeting to the legation staff. I wondered about all the attention being paid to a small consular office in a colony far from the theater of the world war.

They went into Harry Wolfe's office and no one else's, Harry being already ensconced. The meetings lasted for several hours, and when they emerged, the participants looked as if they had been put through a wringer. Though they tried to conceal their fatigue and nerves drawn thin, they were rarely successful. The legation staff saw them twice, once when they arrived and once when they left. Where they were going and what they were about was not the staff's affair. Not at the beginning, but well along, the exception was to be me.

Without warning, I was summoned into the inner sanctum one day by Harry.

"Bob," he said with exaggerated camaraderie, "Can we borrow you for a few minutes?" With a smile still on his face, he whispered, *"Don't ask any questions."*

I did exactly that, compounding it by totally ignoring the latest visitor to the legation. I never forgot the impact he made on me. He was a man with a sphinx face that never changed. He might as well have been cast from stone.

Abandoning even the pretense of cordiality, nobody asked me to take a seat. I stood in the center of the room with their eyes fixed on me. Harry broke the silence by asking a question. "Bob," he said. "Have you seen anything out of the ordinary in the time you've been here?"

I had seen quite a few things out of the ordinary, but never anything that far out. The curious procession of faceless men came to mind, but common sense told me that constant affair was off limits. I said nothing, but I could not keep my eyes from looking at the most recent of the faceless men. If he thought that my reflex was out of the ordinary, he never revealed it. As far as he and I were concerned, he didn't exist.

"There must be something you've noticed," said Harry. "Something that bothered you."

Something that had bothered me suddenly came to mind. "Well, there was something, but it's fixed now. It was the code room."

Harry knew what I was going to say, but the others didn't, and my reference to that sensitive area struck them like a hot needle.

"Go on, Bob," said Doc Pogue in a friendly tone.

I told them. On my first day at the Consulate General, I was given a Cook's tour of building and grounds. Nothing there. The code room was something else.

The code room was located in a screened porch. Code boards were propped open on an easel, and the code officer sat in front of them, so the code man's back and the boards' surfaces were in place for anyone peeking in. I raised my eyes and gasped as if I had been hit in the stomach. The office building next to the legation was a three-story affair with a dozen windows looking at the American legation building, *and* a code room open to the world. Anyone with a telescope or binoculars could read the confidential words that slid across the face of the code board.

"What's the matter?" Harry had asked with an edge of alarm in his voice.

I told him. There was a whitening around his mouth when he led me out of the code room and into his office, where he pounded his desk soundlessly.

When I had finished talking, Harry looked directly into our guest's face. "It's so," said Harry, "and I take full blame for my stupidity. What's worse is that we don't have any idea of how much of what you need could have been discovered by a spy with a telescope. In Bob's time here, we've sent nothing vital to the State Department. Before that, I can't be sure."

I nodded my head and turned to go, but Doc Pogue interrupted me, "I think it's about time we put our cards on the table. Bob, this quiet man here is Paul Cromie. He's attached to the Office of Strategic Services. What the oss does is no secret in the government. It's the intelligence arm of the United States. You might as well know that I'm with the oss, too. Both Paul and I trained under Wild Bill Donovan. You might as well know, too, that we are the last living agents in Donovan's first corps of trainees. Our numbers are just about up, I kid you not. But we knew the odds when we signed on."

Paul Cromie was a sturdily built and handsome man cast in a hardened mold. He stepped across the room to shake my hand. "Sorry for the silent role," he said, "but I've got to be sure who I'm talking to." He paused and then said, "You have to be wondering what all this points to."

"Right. A lot of things aren't clear, but knowing you're espionage helps a lot. But how do I fit in? I don't appreciate not knowing what's going on here, and why."

"Bob, we have to be careful," said Harry Wolfe. "This place is crawling with Nazi spies."

"We wouldn't have told you," Doc Pogue said. "But Paul Cromie and I have a problem. That's where you fit in."

"Our code man is down with the fever. Malaria," said Cromie. "He's out of his head half the time."

"So we have important stuff to send to State," said Paul Cromie. "And nobody to code it."

"You want me to handle your stuff?"

"Yep," said Cromie, "until we can smuggle one of our code men into the Congo operation."

"Of course I will," I said. I stopped and looked at Harry Wolfe, uncertain whether to go on.

"I've told Bob, 'no questions.' That still goes, unless you want to change your mind."

"Young man," said Paul Cromie. "For your own sake, it's better that you don't know."

I walked back to the vice-consul quarters I shared with Harry Wolfe and the economic attaché, Dan Weathers. The two big questions remained unanswered: *Why is the Congo suddenly important enough to be a hotbed of spies? What was here in a dark corner of darkest Africa that was important enough to set American spies at odds with the Belgian government-in-residence?*

Belgian Congo, Africa

"Would you like to go hunting water buffalo?" my Belgian friend Georges asked me.

"Where?"

"On my father's plantation, back in the bush," Georges said. "We get there by boat, about fifty miles down the Congo."

George's invitation came as a welcome diversion for me. I had grown weary of the diplomatic soirées, the same faces and the same conversations. For my private life, I had gone to the lone movie theater in Leopoldville, dated a Belgian girl named Germaine under strict scrutiny of her parents, who did not trust American young men, played tennis at one of the grand houses and grounds in the suburbs, gave Harry Wolfe constant boxing lessons, which he told me he could have used to cope with German insults in the open city of Tangier in Morocco, boxed with my young Belgian friend, Georges Mignon, and was a silent listener at the numerous get-togethers of legation officials and American businessmen and Afrikaners come up from South Africa on export and important import trade. From all these exposures, my command of French improved, though I learned more from talking to the legation's houseboys than anything else.

As to my Belgian friend Georges Mignon's invitation to go hunting, I didn't want to admit that a water buffalo was something alien to me. I didn't even know what one looked like, much less how formidable one could be. When finally I saw a mounted head, I was shaken to the core. His horn spread was easily four feet wide, and his frontal plate looked to be six inches thick. As I learned, that frontal plate could bounce a bullet back from a heavy-caliber gun.

Harry Wolfe and I had talked about forays into the bush, but so far the occasion to go hadn't come up. Naturally, I asked Harry if he wanted to join us on the hunt. Doubtful at first, he decided to take advantage of the rare invitation.

When I brought up the question of guns, Georges assured me the plantation was well equipped. Nevertheless, I used my casual officer influence to borrow a couple of rifles from the American military post just outside of Leopoldville. The rifles when delivered were a little outdated. They were Springfields of World War I vintage. Still, they were heavy rifles, no fooling about that.

At least, we looked the part of *great white hunters*. A shopping trip to an outdoorsman sporting-goods outlet netted us the required pith helmets and bush jackets. Stanley and Livingstone would have approved.

At the dock, we boarded a hand-hewn boat directly across the Congo from Brazzaville, capital of French Equatorial Africa. The city had been occupied by de Gaulle and the Free French, but they were gone now to England.

The boat was carved from heavy hardwood to withstand the force of the river. The Congo is one of the mighty rivers of the world. From eroding banks for God knows how long, the water was brown and filled with silt.

The bulk of the boat was stacked high with hard-to-get provisions and machinery parts for the plantation, bought by Georges in Leopoldville. Georges had no taste for living on a plantation away from white colonists and girls, so he had coerced his father into letting him head up the plantation's business headquarters in Leopoldville. He was good humored and content with his lot in life.

As a hobby, Georges served as a sparring mate for his father, a brute of a man who once had been heavyweight boxing champion of Belgium. At outside social events, he would demonstrate the postures and punches in a classic contest. Georges would make an exaggerated defense. There was no danger in it. Georges's father would not have dared to hit him with the slightest of punches.

The outside dinners and social drinking often looked for diversion to boxing matches between blacks. Though using a boxing style that would have pleased John L. Sullivan, the black fighters were muscular, quick, and adroit, having learned their movements from the exhibitions given by Georges's father.

I talked to them once when I went to a training session. Though I taught them a few feints and hooks, I made the mistake of telling them that a black man, Joe Louis, was heavyweight champion of the world. They were wide-eyed with awe, and I was formally reprimanded and nearly ejected from the Congo for breaching the unspoken code of separation of races. I deserved it. It was one thing for me to find colonial racism on every hand, but it was not for me to breach diplomatic standards of conduct. I was a guest in the country, and I was reminded of that from my first days, when I voiced my disgust at Belgian treatment of Congo natives. Still, I could judge for myself that the Belgians were cruel rulers, the French colonials apathetic about it all, and the British admirable for their gentle treatment of natives. I concluded rightly that blacks regarded the British as their favorite colonials.

Back to our hunting trip for water buffalo:

The heavily laden boat was rowed by six young blacks with powerful arms and shoulders. The muscles that played along their bare backs rippled. Thanks to the rowers, the boat was under their full control in the roaring Congo. They knew the river like the backs of their hands.

The banks of the Congo were thick and tangled and a riot of red, green, and blue colors. The shallow waters along its sides bore lily pads of delicate hues. The giant trees were so interlaced with creepers and vines that I could see how Tarzan had made his flying way through the forests. Nothing diminished the idyllic beauty, except for armor-plated crocodiles slithering into the river.

Our arrival at the plantation dock was not unexpected. I asked Georges how the natives knew of our coming. He shrugged and said it was either the wireless or the jungle drum grapevine that seemed to bear drumbeat messages from one end of Africa to another. I had heard that bit of local color when I first arrived and rejected it as myth. The drums were so numerous in the native quarter of Leopoldville that I rarely went to sleep without hearing their low, muffled rhythm.

When the time came for me to leave Africa, I was not so sure that the drumbeat grapevine was myth. When I was leaving the Consulate General one night, Mbote the errand boy said to me in Swahili French, "Your warriors have invaded the village of the Germans." This momentous news about D-Day did not reach our consulate until the next morning.

There was a throng waiting for us at the plantation's dock. They seemed to be shouting something in unison. I asked Georges what it was they were chanting. He said, "They are saying that the white hunters have arrived."

A venerable old man holding a flintlock rifle stood at the head of the waiting group. Georges said to me, "That is Ikelembote, their chief. Pay him deference."

Harry Wolfe said with an edge of sarcasm, "Do we bow or kneel when we meet him?"

"Treat him with patience," said Georges. "They are but children."

When we climbed up to the dock, the chief and his followers welcomed us. The chief held out his rifle with an awful dignity. Harry took it in his hands. "What in the hell am I supposed to do with it?"

"Inspect it," said Georges. "It is his most prized possession, presented to him by white explorers long ago." Harry's eyes met mine. I said to Harry, "Don't say it." I knew that Harry was thinking that the white explorers were Stanley and Livingstone.

Harry read my plea and said nothing. Instead, he up-ended the flintlock and stared down its barrel. "My God, it looks like a minefield." He handed the rusted old breechloader to me. I nodded in approval and returned it to the chief with a smile.

Georges interrupted the ceremony before it could be prolonged. "The chief will lead us tomorrow on the hunt for water buffalo. He will be armed with that rifle."

"God help us," Harry muttered.

Where the plantation's wheatfields played out and the bush began, Georges gathered everyone around him to give his instructions. When we entered the bush, it would be in single file. Ten natives would go in front, five to hack the way with machetes through the most impenetrable jungle I would ever see, and five spearmen to lead the attack.

Next would come the hunters, Harry and I with our trusty Springfields, Georges and the chief with his ancient flintlock. Five additional spearmen would bring up the rear. I asked Georges why that was necessary, and he responded, "The water buffalo is a clever quarry. He has been known to circle a safari and attack from the rear." Georges was unarmed because hunting did not interest him.

Our stretch of the jungle was bisected by a stream that ran down to the Congo River. Water buffalo would apparently use the stream to reach the river, where they could wallow and play along the way in the mud. They fed on the luxuriant plant life and sometimes made forays into the outer boundaries of the plantation to partake of rich grain.

For our protection from insects, Georges had fashioned a hood of mosquito netting that fit over our pith helmets and covered our faces. It was tied at the throat. We donned gloves so that all our skin surfaces were covered. We had gotten used to living with mosquito netting in Leopoldville. No bed was without it.

Georges's precautions against getting bitten seemed overdone, until we penetrated the Congo bush. A cloud of insects — mosquitoes, flies, and gnats — descended upon us in a whining frenzy, so numerous that we had to brush them off our facial netting in order to see ten feet ahead.

Our native spearmen and hackers and the chief didn't seem to be bothered that much. Generations of malaria had built for them an immunity of sorts in their collective blood streams. But they still suffered from attacks, and sometimes died. For the whites, it was touch-and-go whether they could survive a long siege of fever. The cemetery was filled with the gravestones of Belgians who had come to colonize the Congo in early days and died young.

Progress through the dense jungle had to be measured in feet, nothing approaching a mile in open terrain, so that half the day was consumed just to get to the heart of the bush. Nearby, I had seen the tops of tall trees, and I made my way to the grove to find a temporary escape from insects and overpowering heat that foliage can trap. Though it seemed I had never passed a single day in the Congo without perspiring, everything before was child's play compared to this. The sweat drenched our bodies like a downpour.

There was an hour of respite in the tall trees. They covered this clearing of dirt with a cathedral light. From the log I had found to sit on, I could look up and see the topmost branches so interlaced that little sunlight could penetrate them.

Earth's first days must have looked the same. Instinctively, I reached down and dug a handful of dirt from what had been primeval earth. It felt so old. Now, with each new discovery pointing toward Africa as the birthplace of man, I know it is so.

A sudden clamor of shouting from the safari in the bush shattered my reverie. Reluctantly, I picked up my rifle and headed down to the safari's resting place. Only Harry Wolfe and Georges were still there, showing no signs of impatience with our slow pace and no eagerness to go see what the natives had found. We would learn soon enough. A native spearman was trotting up to the knoll where we were resting. He chattered away in Swahili to Georges.

"They have found tracks of a water buffalo," Georges translated. "The tracks are reasonably fresh. He says that we will find our quarry by midafternoon."

Dragging ourselves to our feet, we went down to the tiny meadow where the natives had found the tracks.

When we got there, I looked down in horror. I had expected the tracks to be like those of a Wisconsin dairy cow. These were literally five times as big. I looked despairingly at Harry and Georges. "We're not following a water buffalo," I said shakenly. "We're on the trail of a dinosaur."

"I think you are dead right," Harry said. "Let's call it a day."

Georges shook his head insistently. "We must pursue the hunt. If we don't, our credibility will be damaged for . . . for . . ."

"Unto the third generation," said Harry.

"Yes, until then at least," said Georges, misunderstanding Harry.

So we rejoined our native escort. Harry was noticeably dragging his feet, while I kept my eyes looking out for a tree I could climb. Ordinarily, I would have been furious at the natives for making so much noise. For sure, they were frightening our quarry away.

Then I understood. The natives knew exactly what they were doing.

So ended our first and only safari trek into the heart of darkest Africa. I had not managed to shoot a monstrous water buffalo, but as I learned later, the tiniest of African denizens got me.

Leopoldville, Belgian Congo, Africa

I had never seen taciturn and unrevealing Doc Pogue in such good humor. All the way from the Consulate General down the tree-lined boulevard to midtown Leopoldville, he had been talking and chortling. I wondered if the fever had gotten to him.

Of course it had not. The jovial nature was only one of the disguises he had learned in OSS training in Washington. I remembered Harry telling me that espionage agents have a well-filled bag of tricks designed to throw counterespionage agents off the track.

There was no shortage of counterspies in Leopoldville. Nazi Germany was making sure of that. They revealed themselves often. Even the most clever of agents is capable of slipping into his native language at the numerous soirées and evening affairs that to me, at least, are a plague upon the diplomatic life. After enduring a round of soirées, I made it a point to avoid them at any excuse. I was not in the business of gathering morsels of information that might fit into the big picture of intelligence gathering. The days of Mata Hari and the BIG SECRET were long past.

For the drink Doc Pogue had invited me to have with him, he chose a table in the middle of the Hotel Metropole's sidewalk café. For the Belgians, it was apéritif time for drinks before dinner, so the sidewalk café was crowded. Doc had called to reserve that particular table. I was to learn the reason not long after drinks were served.

A hum of conversation punctuated by laughter pretty well drowned out what Doc Pogue said to me. With a wide grin on his face, he said, "If what I have to say to you doesn't match the expression on my face, pay it no mind."

Nodding, I grinned back.

"There's been another attempt on my life."

My grin disappeared. It took all my determination to recapture it. "I didn't know there had been *any.*"

"No reason you should," nodded Doc. "In my line of work, it's the name of the game. My fellow spies in Wild Bill's first class are all dead. Cromie told you that."

"What happened to them?"

"Rifle, machine pistols, bombs, and two executions. The North African fireworks under General Mark Clark's little visit alone accounted for two agents. But we had to know if *they* knew he was making a personal visit to brief the Free French for an Allied invasion."

This I had never been aware of, though visitors to the code room at the State Department were throwing Mark Clark's name around carelessly, I now saw.

Doc Pogue threw back his head and laughed.

"We won that round. Mark Clark came in by submarine. He had his meetings and left, again by submarine."

"The others?" I asked, suddenly afraid I was going too far.

"You aren't," said Doc Pogue, reading my mind. "But you're close."

"Why are the Nazis after you now?" I asked, joining Doc Pogue in his laughter. "There's no war here."

"Yes, there is," said Doc. "But not the battlefield category. We're the solitary soldiers with no supporting fire."

I looked my incredulity. "What the heck is going on?"

"If you haven't noticed anything particular in the stuff you're coding for us," said Doc, "we're doing okay."

"I've noticed one thing odd," I said. "Are we in the mining business?"

Doc Pogue was startled. "We might be."

"For what? I know there's gold and diamonds in the Congo, but South Africa is a lot better source than here."

"I think you know enough," said Doc. "Let's leave it right there."

I said the word without thinking. "*Shinkolobwe.*"

"Jesus Christ," said Doc, looking around us at Belgians having a good time. "Don't ever use that word in anybody's presence. Not ever!"

I was chastised. "Don't worry. I won't."

"I've told Harry what I'm going to tell you, without going into detail," Doc Pogue said. "You should know, since you're handling our coded stuff. But for Christ's sake, don't talk about it with anyone."

I nodded soberly.

Doc Pogue said, "You're looking too serious. Start smiling again." His face twisted into a grin. He waited until the hilarity at the next table had risen in volume. Then he leaned forward. "You won't find it in our mining reference reports, so don't bother looking. There's something in that mine that both the United States and Germany want more than anything else in the world. It's in that word I don't want you to repeat, either in Swahili or English. I don't know what it's for. We're not supposed to know. I doubt whether the German agents here know, either."

I said with sincerity, "I'm not sure I want to find out."

"I'll tell you what its name is, because you will probably never know what it's used for," said Doc Pogue.

"But if you don't know, what's the sense in trying to kill you?"

"Because they think I've discovered something, and they want it kept quiet, absolutely quiet," said Doc Pogue. He leaned back as if he were giving a lecture. Which he was. "The Shinkolobwe mine contains a mineral called uranium. The Congo has the only producing mine."

He said the word without emotion. Years later, I was to remember that.

"Until 1940," he went on, "nobody attached any importance to the word or the mineral. Our mining people considered it worthless. Its main value was in coloring glass and for whatever little radium and silver it contained. Still, the Germans must have known there was something else in there. Until 1940, they were just about the only importer of uranium. We would just have thrown it away."

What he was saying struck a bell with me. "Back in 1860, in my state of Nevada, prospectors had to cope with a black mud that was hindering them in their search for gold. Then somebody took the trouble to have the black mud assayed in California. It turned out to be the richest silver ore in recorded history." I told the story to Doc Pogue.

Doc Pogue thought a while. "That may be the case here. The scientists may have discovered another use for uranium." He went on with what he had been relating. "When Hitler invaded Belgium in 1940, the Belgians cut off their Congo source, which turned out to be pure stuff. Our intelligence must have stumbled on to what the real value was in uranium. That's when our country began buying and importing the stuff in carloads. That's sent to enrichment plants to make it purer. Don't ask me 'purer for what.' The Germans are trying to get all the uranium the Congo can produce. There's a deep dark suspicion that King

Leopold is waiting to see who's winning the war—Hitler or us. He'll throw all the Congo uranium to us if our side is going to win the war."

"What about you?"

"They think I've discovered something, and they want to squelch it by killing me."

"You could always send it in code."

"They probably don't trust codes. For that matter, neither do we. So that leaves the only other alternative—killing the source."

"Do you really know something they don't?"

"That question is what I mean by going too far," said Doc Pogue, his face closing down into its sphinx cast.

SEPTEMBER, 1944

Leopoldville, Belgian Congo, Africa

Doc Pogue had disappeared.

When by midmorning Doc had not shown up for a meeting with Harry Wolfe, he called Doc's number at the bungalow where he lived. There was no answer. We saw later where the telephone line had been neatly cut.

Though Doc despised such displays, Harry and I and Weathers were getting ready to drive to the bungalow. Harry had invited Weathers along because he was big and burly, which meant he expected trouble. We were going out the back door to the Consulate General when Joselle, our secretary, called us back.

The Belgian gendarmerie was on the line. That news confirmed Harry's suspicion that something out of the ordinary had happened. It had, and the gendarmerie had been aware of it for at least three hours. They had been alerted by Doc's houseboy, who worked days cleaning and gardening at the bungalow. Harry's voice rose in incredulity. The response must have been lame, because Harry slammed the telephone down.

"Let's go," Harry said in a controlled voice. "Doc's bungalow has been shot apart, and there's no trace of him." The houseboy, who slept in the native quarter, had walked right through an open front door.

Harry braked to a squealing stop in the alleyway that ran alongside the bungalow. There was only one Belgian gendarme inside. No detective squad searching for evidence, dusting for fingerprints, as in the United States or by the French Sureté.

The living room looked undamaged, but the bedroom door had been broken down. Just inside the door, there was a pool of blood that led out the kitchen door and into the alleyway. We found these without a helping word from the gendarme.

Doc's bedroom looked like a small war had been fought there during the night. Hanging lamps, a clock, and pottery were in fragments, and the wall beside Doc's bed was pockmarked with bullet holes. But what was most curious was that Doc's mattress had been tipped over toward the wall like a protecting buffer. Obviously, it had served as a shield for Doc when the shooting started. To our vast relief, coupled with puzzlement, there was not a drop of blood behind the mattress.

Harry Wolfe confronted the gendarme. There were some questions that needed answering. "Then the first you knew of your famous *incident,* as you call it, was when the houseboy brought you here?" Harry asked in a strangled voice. "Did your people take Mr. Pogue's body away? What about the *assassin?*" Harry purposely emphasized the word.

"No bodies," said the gendarme. "Nor noise.

Obviously, they used silencers," he added in a superior tone.

"Well, thank God for that," said Harry. "At least there's a chance Doc is alive."

"What about shell casings?" Weathers said. "Were the assassin's bullets dug out of that wall for evidence?"

"I have the shell casings here," the gendarme said, smugly patting his side pocket.

"Can we see them?" said Weathers. "I know something about guns and bullets."

The gendarme shook his head. "They are the gendarmerie's evidence."

"What kind of a gun did the assassin use?" said Weathers.

"That is not for me to say," said the gendarme.

"Will there be an investigation?"

"Of course," the gendarme said. "There has been a shooting here. We will discover who was involved."

"I'll bet you will," Harry muttered in an undertone.

"Didn't the neighbors see or hear anything?" I asked. "There had to be things like voices and cars and a door being smashed."

The gendarme regarded me as if I were an ignorant child. "Even if they did, Belgians would say nothing. They don't want to be involved with *espions,* which these people obviously are."

"At least Doc nailed the sonofabitch," said Weathers. "That's a lot of blood back there."

Harry started to press again for the shell casings from the gunman's weapon. It would have been in vain. I leaned over to whisper in Harry's ear. "Forget him. I'm standing on one."

The gendarme was taking his leave. We didn't bother to say goodbye. I handed the shell casing to Harry. He looked it over and handed it to Weathers. Weathers twirled the casing around in his fingers. "What I figured," he said. "A machine pistol. Mauser. That spells an SS killer. Machine pistols aren't accurate, but they can spit out a lot of bullets in a hurry." He waved his hand at the pock-marked wall. "That's what I mean."

"And Doc?" I asked. "He showed his gun to me once, but only for a second. It was flat as a pancake and just about as thick. I was disappointed."

"You shouldn't have been," said Weathers. "That crude little toy has killed more spies than any machine pistol. It's a single-shot .45. The shooter has one chance to hit. At close range, the impact is devastating."

"If you miss?" asked Harry.

"You're done for, of course," said Weathers. "But Wild Bill Donovan's spy people had better be dead shots." He pointed at the pool of blood beside the broken bedroom door. "Doc didn't miss."

We followed the trail of blood left by the SS killer. It led out the kitchen door. There must have been a car waiting there for him. The trail led to the driver's seat, then circled the car to the passenger side and stopped there.

A search of Doc's drawers and closet yielded nothing of value. We were familiar with his wardrobe, and it all seemed to be where it was supposed to be. Even personal toiletries such as razors and a toothbrush seemed to be in their proper places. Drawers were not disturbed. We inspected the desk with a fine-tooth comb. All that it contained of any possible importance was a routine report on the mining activities at Shinkolobwe.

It was as though Doc Pogue had vanished into thin air. He was either dead, or he had managed somehow to get away. It would be some time before we knew the answer to that riddle.

Leopoldville, Belgian Congo, Africa

There is no sense in kidding myself. I have malaria. It has been coming on ever since our botched-up hunting trip through the bush and swamps of Georges Mignon's family plantation. Mignon's complicated mosquito netting couldn't keep Annie away from me. Among the English and Americans, *Annie* is short for *Anopheles,* the tiny deadly mosquito that preys on man. . . .

Four or five days ago—I lost a day somewhere—I was working in the code room with the pounding headache I had wakened to. Aspirin did no good whatever.

Though it was midday and suffocatingly hot and humid, I felt a chill starting deep inside me. No one else in the Consulate General seemed to be affected. Shirts and blouses were plastered with sweat to bare skin, except for me. My forehead and hands were dry and cold to the touch.

I tried to ignore the growing chill, but in a matter of minutes, I was shaking like a leaf. No one seemed to notice except for our Swahili errand boy, Mbote. He dropped the code room's mail—personal letters in one basket and official letters in another—then picked up our routine mail to other consulates. He went to the door and suddenly stopped and looked back, as if trying to remember something that had caught his attention. That something was me.

He padded back to my coding board and looked down intently at me. He did an abrupt about-face and shuffled through the door into the Consulate General's waiting room. Mbote didn't bother knocking on Harry's door, but walked right in. There was a muffled reprimand from Harry, silence, and then Harry's hurried footsteps.

"Holy Christ! You've got it."

He didn't have to say more. Everyone knew what "it" meant.

Ordering Weathers to close up shop in the code room, Harry took my arm and propelled me out the back doorway to his car.

By the time we reached the vice-consul's quarters, I was shivering so badly I couldn't form an understandable word. One of the vice-consul's houseboys, Antoine, ran out to meet us. On his face, he wore an expression of much concern. He had had his experience with malaria, too.

That African blacks are immune to malaria is the white man's myth. Quinine is expensive, and there are ten million blacks in Africa. If a native doesn't die from malaria when he is a child, he builds up a certain amount of immunity, but that is all. I saw too many natives with flaming red eyes and chattering teeth to believe otherwise. Whenever one of them in the compound was bad off, I would dose him with quinine, against all rules. One dose alone would cut the attack short.

Antoine and Harry half carried me to my bed and put me in it, clothes and all. "Blankets!" said Harry. "Pile every blanket you can find over him. It won't do anything to stop the freezing, but he will think it does."

Sometime in the night, the chills left me, only to be replaced by the coming of fever. This part of the cycle still brings nightmares to me. The fever is insidious, working its way to the "onslaught of pestilence" that historians write about. It is accompanied by burning thirst, pain, and delirium. For the fever, Harry dosed me with bitter quinine. For the thirst, Antoine poured water down me in cascades. For the pain, I could do nothing. For the delirium, even less. Harry, who stayed the night sitting for the most part in a chair, told me I was babbling about snow-topped mountains, blue skies, and cool Sierra forests, bleating sheep and lambs, barking dogs, and the small canvas tent that was my father's shelter. My dreams began to show me where my heart belonged, and it was not in steaming Africa. Anger against my country was waning.

I became aware in a strange way of the passage from fever to the final stage of my first attack of malaria. In the months that followed, it was to become a familiar transition.

During the fever, I was to become more familiar with one phenomenon of an attack than with the others. It was a sensation that is difficult to describe. The first time, I was lying flat on my back as the fever rose in intensity. My arms were at my sides, on top of the cotton blanket that covered me. I was looking at their backs. Something was happening there that I couldn't make out, except that the skin covering my face and hands felt and looked dry and brittle.

When my curiosity could be contained no longer, I put one hand on top of the other. I remember recoiling. It was like touching parchment. I felt that I could pinch the skin of my hands and it would crackle and tear like paper. With an exclamation of disgust, I raised my hands until they were right in front of my eyes. With their creases and lines, they were an old man's hands. I jerked them down and plunged them under my blanket so that they were concealed from my consciousness.

When the attack went into its final stage, however, it was my hands that told me what was coming.

Except for two months or so in the dry season, which is called the cold season—by comparison, I suppose—the Congo can only be described as hot and humid. One is bathed in sweat all night and all day. I had become so inured to it that there were times when I took it for granted.

But when my fever passed, the heat was so intense and the humidity so wet and close that I thought I would suffocate. I had never felt anything like it before.

My hands were at my sides again. I looked down at them, realizing that something had changed. They were not an old man's hands anymore, but soft with moisture. As I watched, I saw something like a blister rise from the surface of my hand, swell and burst. Then came other blisterlike bubbles, until the perspiration was running in little rivers onto the cotton cover.

As I was to learn, this was the purging stage of an attack. In a matter of minutes, my body was so drenched that I felt as though I were lying in a pool of my own sweat. I gave a shout and then another. Antoine's bare feet slapped on the stone floor.

"Good sign," he said. "Good sign. Body washing away malaria. Pretty soon, you sleep."

Antoine was right. When the burning heat had scoured the last traces of the fever away, I fell into a deep and peaceful sleep, for how many hours I can't remember. When I awakened, Harry was standing over me. He put his hand on my brow and said, "All normal, Bob. Annie Anopheles is napping, getting ready for the next go-round. Why don't you get rested up, too? You'll need it. When you wake up, I'll have broth waiting for you." He paused at the door and said, "By the way, you look like hell."

Belgian Congo, Africa

Mail from home has come all in a bunch. Thank God for that. It must have piled up at one of the A.P.O.s either in San Francisco or Miami. I was beginning to think everyone had forgotten me. . . .

October, 1944
Carson City, Nevada

Dear Robert,

I am ashamed for not having answered to your letters before this, but you know how my life is going between trailing the sheep and going to town for provisions when I think the sheep will be safe and not scatter too much. I don't worry about the coyotes because my two sheep dogs are big and good fighters. If coyotes talk to each other, they know that Jumbo and Barbo will kill them pretty damn quick.

Summer grazing is over and I am driving the ewes and lambs to where the livestock trucks will pick them up and send them to fattening yards and then to market. I kept 100 lambs to build for next year's yearling band. Them and the old ewes will make 2,000 head, which is not much.

The lambs did good in the high mountains this summer. They are fat and should bring a good price, but it was not easy herding them to where the good feed was. How I could have used you and Paul to help me out, getting provisions from town, herding a little and counting the sheep to see if any were missing. Robert, I wish you had taken that livestock exemption from the Armed Force, but you had your mind made up and nobody could change it.

I still can't find any help at all. You know the Basque boys from France and Spain can't come to America anymore, and what Americans there are around are next to useless. They are mostly Irish and Scotch, and when they get fed up being alone, they just walk off and go to town to get drunk. A Basque herder would die before deserting the sheep. I will make it somehow until the sheep are in winter range in the Ramsey desert and I can leave them alone for a few hours when I go to town to get provisions.

Mama and the rest of the family here are fine, but she worries about you. Not much family here now and getting less. I cannot bring up the words to tell you about your sister, so I will let her tell you in her own words.

> *Ikus Artio,*
> Hoping this will reach you —
> Your Aita

Dear Bob,

As you probably have guessed, I have a ringside seat for the biggest show on earth, the invasion of the Philippines. It was really something, and even tho we caught holy hell and are still catching it, I'm sort of glad that I managed to get in on it. If I do get out okay, and there's no reason I shouldn't now, it will really be worth remembering. I've had so many close shaves that I feel a lot like a cat with nine lives now. I guess that when we first hit the beach, it was the worst, but now that I look back on it, I can see how lucky I was to get out okay. We no sooner hit when we ran into a bunch of snipers and all hell broke loose. From then on, it was one big nightmare after another until lately when things have cooled down somewhat. The snipers are almost all knocked out, and air raids are our only worry. You'd get a big thrill out of seeing one of the "Bettys" or "Zeros" get shot down. When one does get it, and it's a pretty frequent occurrence, everyone cheers like hell and sounds like the Cal and Stanford rooting sections put together. It isn't so funny tho, when they drop a few eggs or do a strafe job. We just hole up and pray like the devil. You ought to see the number of atheists turn Christian all of a sudden when we have a close shave. That saying about no atheists in foxholes is certainly true.

Enough about me. I hope you have come to your senses and asked the State Department for an extended sick leave. You can't be doing them or your country any good with that load of malaria and whatever else you are carrying around. If they turn down your request (but I can't see how they could), write to the Senator. He'll get you home in a hurry.

Hopefully, I'll be seeing you before too long, so until then let's keep our fingers crossed. I feel before two years are up, we'll be together again, and a wiser, happier group we'll be.

Your brother,
Paul

Bob dear:

Do you remember that September morning when we looked at each other across our horses and said, "That's enough range riding for today. To hell with work. Let's hie away, as Bobby Burns would say, and go joy riding to our garden spot looking down on the desert"?

I swung by the kitchen and picked up some lunch things and we took off at a dead run. A rain shower caught us, but we didn't care. We had our slickers to keep us dry. When we got to the spring, it had stopped raining and the desert was redolent with the scent of sage after a storm.

This is why I have enclosed a sprig of sagebrush in my letter. I could talk forever about the desert and the sagebrush, but nothing can match the actual scent of it.

Do you remember sitting on our slickers and making a ground cover to eat our Basque lunch—*Ogi eta gazna eta arnua*. Bread and cheese and wine.

My sisters and I are doing all the buckarooing for the ranch now. There are no good cowboys to be had, what with the draft. Mama says we need a man around the ranch, now that Papa is dead. Who do you think she means? But I keep telling her that we haven't made up our minds. When the

73

war is over and we decide what to do with our lives, we can make our decision about marriage.

Until then, with God's help, rid yourself of malaria. May the scent of sage tell you where your home is.

Bihotzez,
Pilar

November, 1944
Carson City, Nevada

Bien cher Robert:

We just receive your letter about the malaria. I am so worried. What is happening to our family?

Suzette is gone to convent. In her order, the nuns are what they call cloistered. It is like a daughter dying.

Paul is in the fighting in the Pacific and you are sick in Africa from the malaria. And John is in the Navy, but safe.

I pray every morning at Holy Mass that my sons will come home safe. I could not bear it if I lose you two, too. Our dinner table is nearly empty now, with your little brother, Mick, and your little sister, Marie, the only ones to cook for except when your father can come home from the hills for a day. It is a sad thing to see.

En attendant de tes bonnes nouvelles. Nous t'embrassons. N'oublie pas le messe de dimanche.

Your mother

San Francisco, California

My dear brother in Christ:

You have probably heard from the whole family by now of the decision I have made. I think you will be either angry with me, or sad.

I want you to know that the decision to join the order was mine alone. I have done what I have done out of my own free will.

Actually, it should not come as that much of a surprise. In your heart, you must know that this was what my life was pointing to from the very beginning.

Even then, the choice I made was not an easy one. I was in torment for so long a time. Not about my vocation, but about the timing of it. You in the Congo (and sick from malaria, I have just learned), Paul in combat and by his own words, wondering when and if his luck would run out.

I will make a confession once and for all. I was so worried about my dear brothers that I almost made a pact with God. Unless He spared your lives and brought you home safe, I would not enter the order. Then I realized that I had committed a terrible sacrilege even thinking such a thing. My mind was made up at that instant.

When I told them, Papa was in tears and Mama thankfully was resigned to my doing what I must do.

My decision was the right one. When I heard those iron doors close behind me, my heart was not sad. Wistful, maybe, but content with the knowledge that my bridegroom would be Blessed Jesus.

Please understand me, and love me. I will love and pray for you both all the days of my life.

Your sister in Christ,
Suzette

Leopoldville, Belgian Congo, Africa

The word *overseas* has lost its glamour for me. Every letter from home was like a drawstring pulling me back to where I belonged—*my country,* right or wrong. I have learned a lot in this experience, but the experience is done with and I am tired of it. This war has shattered our ordered family life, and all I want is to help put that order together again with my loved ones. The foolish things one does in an outrage!

Belgian Congo, Africa

Doc Pogue is alive. Not only alive and well, but safely back home in the United States. . . .

The news came to us by way of a diplomatic courier from the State Department in Washington. There had been no word from Doc through the code route, nor had we expected any. By then, we were convinced he was either dead or carrying a heavy secret. We were pretty certain it had to do with Union Minière's Shinkolobwe mine, where we and the Germans were scrabbling about the uranium for what use nobody seemed to know anything.

The courier opened the diplomatic pouch with an impressive key attached to a silver chain he wore around his neck. The key was accompanied on the same chain by a Saint Christopher's medal.

The courier was crew-cut, muscular, and military in his bearing. He had been a lieutenant in the Marine Corps, but a back injury in his first action had cut short his military career. Too energetic for a desk job, he had become a courier for the State Department, a venture not lacking for excitement. A manacle linked the diplomatic pouch to the courier's wrist. The pouch itself was a sturdy leather and canvas affair whose scars showed how widely it had traveled.

The courier upended the pouch on Harry's conference table and then took off his khaki jacket to reveal a tight-fitting shoulder holster with the thinnest and flattest automatic pistol I had ever seen. We had expected he would be carrying the gun, but we were not prepared for the wicked double-edged knife strapped to the underside of his left arm.

"The knife isn't show-off stuff," the courier said to me when he saw I was interested. "If a man knows how to use it, a knife can save him at close quarters better than a gun ever could." He added gratuitously, "The mountain men Indian fighters proved that in hand-to-hand fighting a long time ago."

Parting the mail and dispatches jumbled together on the table, the courier reached for two letters bound by a thick rubber band. "These are special," he said. "One for the second-in-command, Mr. Wolfe, and one for the youngest American in the legation, which I assume is you." He handed the letters individually to Harry and me. "They were given to me to deliver personally by a Mr. Pogue, who works for a man named Wild Bill Donovan, who you may have heard about." He paused for emphasis and added, "Mr. Pogue asks that you read your letters on receipt and then burn them."

It was not government business, but I wanted to know. "How does Mr. Pogue look?"

"At ease with the world," said the courier and added smiling, "I didn't think you wanted to know about what make of suit he was wearing." He thought for a moment and then said, "Actually, he didn't tell me a damned thing except that he used to work here. Here and at some mine neither he nor anybody else in authority wants to talk about." He turned away and began sorting the dispatches and letters for Harry, muttering almost to himself. "I've never seen such a hush-up job. Has to be the best-kept secret in the war."

"We can't help you, either," said Harry and re-treated to his desk to read Doc Pogue's letter. I did the same, pulling a chair to the far corner of the office.

Dear Bob—

My letters to you and Harry Wolfe are essentially the same. If you two want to compare notes, please feel free to do so.

I must apologize for leaving you without a formal adieu. Circumstances made it necessary to make a hasty departure. After two attempts on my life, I knew there would be a third. *Jamais deux sans trois,* as the French say.

I regret having to miss the farewell teas and end-less soirées along Legation Row whenever a rep-resentative of another country leaves. One must sacrifice for the good of the Foreign Service.

My leaving in such haste was not without preparation. I set to work the day after the first attempt with the bomb failed. I knew my cover was blown. It would only be a matter of time. As it turned out, I stayed too long after the try with a knife in the back. But there was one leak at Shinkolobwe I had to try for before I left. I got it and if it checks out, it was worth the try.

It took some talking and a bundle of money (always take money), but I found an old French merchant mariner who had retired to a shabby little houseboat on the Congo. He fished for El Capitan mostly to help supplement his income. I made an arrangement with him to take me downriver to the port at Matadi. Short notice and probably at night. I left a handbag with him just in case—change of clothes, toothbrush, and such.

My biggest worry with him was his drinking. He was a wino. He swore he could navigate the little houseboat drunk or sober, which he probably could. I showed him my gun and told him I would kill him if he got drunk and popped off in a wine shop.

That night, I had a hunch they would try (one develops a sixth sense in this game). That's why I locked the bedroom door. I heard their Mercedes drive into the alleyway, pulled the mattress down to protect me from what I was pretty sure would be coming my way. Then I lay down on the floor with my pistol ready.

I didn't have to wait long. The SS sonofabitch hit the door like a battering ram. He came through shooting. I took my time. With only one shot, you can get awfully careful. That big .45 slug took him in the belly and threw him back out the door. When he got up, I thought I was done for, but he went down again and started crawling toward the kitchen, grunting like a pig. Sorry I can't be charitable about someone trying to kill me.

I heard the Mercedes take off. I didn't wait around. The only thing I took with me was my gun and, most important, my money belt.

I ran all the way to the dock and jumped into the riverboat. The Frenchman shoved off, and we let the current take us downriver until we were out of earshot of town. Then he started up the engine, and we went as fast as the old bucket could take us to Matadi. We got there just before day was breaking. I gave the old Frenchman a handful of bills and warned him to keep quiet about our trip. I think he will, for now at least.

At Matadi, I walked down the docks to the room where my second and last contact lived. He had a list ready with the line and departure dates of Scandinavian freighters heading for the United States. My luck held up. There was a Swedish freighter leaving in two days. The night before, my contact and I went to a bistro where we met with a sailor from the freighter. Some more money changed hands, and I was stowed away on the ship. I lived in a corner of the hold that had been set up with a cot, water, fruit, and bread.

That was my house for two days. Then I went topside, found the captain, and gave him my passport and identification papers. He was a Swede with no love for the Germans. From then on, I was a passenger. Because there are still German subs crawling around the Atlantic, we went straight to Brazil, or rather wove our way to Brazil, the nearest point of land, then followed the coastline all the way to New York. I was home free.

One last bit of advice. Don't ask any questions about Shinkolobwe, and take money.

I won't be going overseas again this war. No regrets. I will see you next in beautiful, safe Washington, D.C. How good is it to be back home.

Doc Pogue

Harry Wolfe and I burned our letters in an incense urn in his office. There was really nothing to say. Harry was probably thinking about the implications of Shinkolobwe. And I was thinking about what Doc had said about how good it was to be back home. I have to believe Doc's words were meant for me. He must have sensed my internal conflict and decided to tell me what *home* meant to him. I am sure I know now what it means to me.

Leopoldville, Belgian Congo, Africa

I was a witness today at the marriage of Harry
Wolfe, whose fiancée is in distant Spain. . . .

The Catholic Church was impressive with two
stories and a steeple rising against the primitive
background of Congo bush. In the afternoon gloom,
Harry and I knelt inside.

Except for the sanctuary lamp bathing the ornate
altar with a red glow, the only light filtered through
the stained-glass windows far above.

Nuns in white habits walked softly up and down
the aisles, bearing flowers of myriad colors to the
altar. They were preparing the church for Christmas, which was only a day away.

Children's voices, soprano and sweet, spilled
down from the choir above. Even though their native tongue was Swahili, their accents were in per-
fect Latin, drummed into them by missionary
priests. Why this never ceases to amaze me I cannot explain. Somehow, civilized and ancient Latin
does not seem to fit with black faces with tribal
markings and sharpened white teeth. Still, their
choral hymns were beautiful, even through there
were interruptions when the choirmaster priest
made them repeat a refrain when they faltered or

sang off-key. They also were preparing for High Mass on Christmas Day.

Unbeknownst to them, they were also casting a religious aura over our private ceremony-to-be.

A week before, Harry had asked me if I would be a witness to his marriage with María. I was nonplussed because the last I knew, María was still in Spain. "Has María come all the way here? When is the wedding to be, and where?"

"Right here in the Congo and at a private chapel in Andalucia. At 5 P.M. on the day before Christmas," he said in a voice that said there had been conversation enough.

I knew parts of the story of Harry Wolfe and María. When he was stationed in Madrid, he had fallen in love with a girl from Spain, daughter of a wealthy Spanish vintner from Andalucia. They were to be married on the day before Christmas three years before. Plans for the wedding were cut short by war between the Axis powers and the United States.

Although Spain had declared its neutrality, it was a fact known by all that General Francisco Franco, the dictator-to-be, was a friend and ally of Adolf Hitler. This fact had been manifest during the Spanish Civil War when Franco was a combatant out to seize power in Spain. When Hitler told him that his Luftwaffe needed practice in bombing real targets, Franco had invited the German air force to bomb a peaceful Basque village named Guernica. The Luftwaffe's Condor Legion did so, pouring death and destruction down on an unarmed village. The devastation was to inspire Picasso's painting, *Guernica*.

When Franco became dictator in Spain and the lines had been drawn for World War II, there was no chance that María's father would permit her marriage to an American. Franco's wrath would come down on the entire family. They would be stripped of everything they owned and possibly jailed in punishment.

Harry and María were left with no alternative but to postpone their formal wedding until the war was ended. Harry was posted to Africa while María remained in Spain.

But their love was not to be frustrated. They exchanged letters through the international city of Tangier. They set a date for a spiritual exchange of marriage vows. Now, that day was here.

Harry strode to the sanctuary railing, kneeled, and bowed his head in silent prayer. Then he raised his eyes to the Christ figure on the altar and said aloud:

"I, Harry, take thee, María, for my lawful wife, to have and to hold from this day forward, for better or for worse, for richer for poorer, in sickness and in health, until death do us part."

Harry kneeled in silence, as though hearing María's voice. Then he crossed himself and, beckoning to me, left the church. We went out into the fading light. The ceremony was never mentioned by either of us again.

Two lives separated by war had been joined at two separate altars in two separate countries.

DECEMBER 28, 1944

Leopoldville, Belgian Congo, Africa

I got up today for the first time since Christmas, which was three lost days ago. . . .

Christmas in the Congo differed in style among the represented countries along Legation Row: Belgium, the United States, England, South Africa, Free France, and even Spain in a token way.

Our only common tie for Christmas was Christianity. Not wanting to chance offending any country, our consul general, J. Wesley Hale, decided to have an American Christmas for his staff. Since we rarely saw him because of his involvement with policy matters and social relations, the Christmas cocktail hour and dinner at his personal mansion promised to be a treat.

The consul general's Christmas festivity had been arranged by his number-one native *boy.* His name was Patrice, and he was already a legend along Legation Row. Tall for a Congolese native, he dressed in stiffly starched uniform coat and trousers. Despite his stylized western attire, he was by his own preference barefoot. Patrice was fluent in half a dozen languages, an expert in mathematics and money, and unequaled in black-market trading. If anyone along Legation Row wanted something unattainable, Patrice would attain it, for a commission. As a result, he was wealthy by native standards and, if the truth were known, probably by white standards. Everyone agreed that Patrice had a future in the Congo.

Our Christmas party began well enough with cocktails on an upraised patio festooned with decorations. Tiny Santa Clauses abounded but missed the mark, since they bore a strong Congolese influence. The highlight was a reasonable facsimile of an Anglo-Saxon Christmas tree glittering with, of all things, American tinsel, compliments of Patrice.

Cocktails were Scotch, Irish gin, and Dry Sack sherry, which put everyone in a jolly mood by the time we stepped down to the garden for dinner. While we were on the veranda, electrically powered fans kept the insect world at bay, but dinner in an open-air garden with the coming of night, and no fans, was a different matter. A cloud of African insects sat down to table with us. When the candles were lighted, snowy white tablecloths were instantly crawling with an insect carpet in hues of black, brown, red, green, gray, and so on. Nevertheless, we sat down to dinner. We had no other choice.

When dinner was served, a curious phenomenon occurred. Our apprehension about eating mouthfuls of food well sprinkled with bugs was turning off appetites before a single fork was raised. But not a single insect settled on the plates. They kept to their own domain on the tablecloths.

Someone ventured a mouthful of salad and pronounced it free of insects. Others followed. So it went throughout the remainder of dinner. For diversion, I watched fascinated as a green mantis five inches long prayed in front of my plate, and a ten-inch benevolent bug with a swivel neck turned his little round head from left to right, following what my hands were doing.

The insect world's politeness ended with the end of dinner. Before the servants could take our plates away, the cloud descended upon china and servers alike. It was as if the servants and the food, being African, were fair game. But Christmas dinner had been a success, and the gathering trooped back up to the patio for coffee and cognac and stories from the guest of honor.

He was a tall, gaunt American named Putnam who was related to a New York publishing company. He had come to Africa with his father years before on a hunting expedition in the classic safari manner. They had penetrated the stygian darkness of the Congo bush that is inhabited by pygmies. Putnam described his near-fatal brush with a bush elephant.

"He was on me so fast, coming out of that concealment of bush, that I had no time to get ready to shoot. I turned to run away when he caught me with his tusks and threw me twenty feet away." Putnam took off his shirt to show the scar carved by the elephant's tusk. It was a deep groove stretching diagonally across his back from hip to shoulder. "I was saved by a Belgian hunter with the longest elephant gun I have ever seen, almost twenty feet long. It took two natives to hold up the barrel. The gun blew a hole the size of a watermelon through my elephant."

Putnam's description of lying bleeding in the bush was graphic. "Within minutes, my whole body was covered with insects—some come to bite, others to suck my blood, and others to lay eggs in the crevices of my flesh."

Putnam said that he would most certainly have died if it had not been for the pygmies. They carried him to their village, threw together an outsized hut to protect him, then treated him with native ointments, keeping him free of infection until he was healed.

"I fell in love with the little people and vowed to stay there with them to learn about their habits and how they have managed to survive in a jungle filled with killer elephants, leopards, and malarial swamps."

Perhaps it was his description of insects devouring him when he lay bleeding, or more likely it was merely timing. Weathers was the first one to stand up and excuse himself. He was shaking like a leaf, and we knew he was having an attack of malaria. "Sorry," he said, "but Annie cares not for Christmas. Happy holidays to you all." He left the patio and was whisked away to the vice-consul's compound before the fever could set in. The consul general could only shake his head in sympathy.

Then Harry, who by this time was also a victim of malaria, got to his feet and promptly crumbled to the floor. He looked like a ghost. The consul general was going to call for a doctor, but Harry, who had recovered consciousness, asked to be taken home instead, since there was little the doctor could do.

"I'll take him home and put him to bed," I said. I couldn't tolerate making the consul general's Christmas party a fiasco by announcing that I too felt the malaria chill coming on.

Commandeering the services of Patrice, we took Harry to his quarters and the skilled treatment his houseboy would give him. When Patrice and I got back into the car, Patrice said, "You are not fooling me. Now it's your turn to go to bed. I know your history of malaria. You are worse off than the other two." His voice dropped to a low warning tone. "You had better go home to America before you die."

Leopoldville, Belgian Congo, Africa

The months of January and February are pretty well lost to me. All I can do is try to make some order out of the scribbles I made when I was rational enough.

JANUARY — As if the malaria weren't enough, I have picked up yellow jaundice. It has turned me a sick yellow. I can't even have a drink, just when I was acquiring a taste for Scotch.

JANUARY — Today was the first time in a week that I haven't come out of a sound sleep in the early morning with a blinding, pounding headache, having to throw up everything in my stomach.

JANUARY — Since my last attack, the malaria has gotten so bad that I'm practically living on quinine. I can't seem to shake it.

FEBRUARY — I'm in terrible shape now. I have amoebic dysentery. I weigh no more than 120 pounds, down from 155. I can count my ribs.

FEBRUARY — The consul general has been transferred to another post. Harry Wolfe is acting consul general now. Lacking an OK to send me home for treatment, he is trying to arrange for a plane to take me to the Kivu Mountains, where it is high and cool.

FEBRUARY—The doctor from Luxembourg has said that he would not be responsible (for my death) if I am not sent home or to a nonmalarial post immediately.

MARCH—We cannot seem to get an answer from State calling me home. Harry has advised me to write my U.S. Senator, McCarran, to light a fire.

MARCH—It worked. I have received cabled orders to return to the United States for debriefing and treatment.

Now that I was going home, my friend Harry had a talk with me.

He said, "Why this hate you have on for the United States?"

I fumbled and stumbled and finally told him the story of my rejections and ridicule, of how my country had diminished me.

Harry said, "Your country hurt you, but it hasn't diminished you." When I didn't answer, he said, "Have you gotten the mad out of your system?"

"I think so. I know so."

"I hope so," said Harry.

Matadi, Africa

Last night was a near thing for me. Today, I am ashamed even to admit it. When I reached my room on the eighth floor of the Hotel Métropole, I took a shower to wash off the day's perspiration. Before I dressed, I went to the full-length mirror in my room and took a look at myself. I was shocked and revolted by what I saw—a hollowed-out face, yellow skin, and thinning hair, all my ribs protruding, pipestem arms and legs. I said in a despairing voice, "I can't go home looking like this. I don't want my family or anyone to see what a mess I am. I just can't face them."

My room fronted on the atrium that penetrated the hotel from the top story to ground floor. In my absolute despair, I put on shirt and trousers and asked God for forgiveness. I was going to throw myself over the railing. At the last minute, I backed away and went into my room and threw myself on my bed and prayed until my crisis had passed.

The African Shore

I said goodbye to the Belgian Congo today. I am on a Swedish freighter going down the coast of Africa to Lobito, where cargo will be unloaded and new cargo put on board. The freighter is hugging the white sand shore with its unbroken background of green, green bush. From Lobito, the freighter will make a zig-zag dash at full speed of twelve knots across the Atlantic. The captain explained that this was necessary because there were still German submarines prowling the Atlantic. In fact, the freighter that left before us was torpedoed at sea. We were to keep on the lookout for survivors. Even this close to shore, we are required to wear life belts all our waking hours.

On leaving Africa

We are on the open sea and Africa is fading into the distance. My mind is filled with recollections of goodbyes to Harry and my people at the Consulate General. Part of my trip from Leopoldville to Matadi was by boat. I floated down that mighty river and watched in wonderment the green banks filled with a voluptuous riot of brilliantly colored equatorial flowers.

Africa is so beautiful. I am sorry that it wasn't for me.

Off of Africa

My health is improving with every day at sea. The captain has given me permission to sprawl out on top of the wheel house ostensibly to look for survivors from the torpedoed freighter, but really to drink up sunshine and lungfuls of sea air. I had forgotten what it was like to breathe air that was not sodden with humidity and filled with microscopic insects.

Mid Atlantic

There was a burial at sea today. A young Swedish sailor died from an attack of malaria. Huge doses of quinine could not save him.

For the burial service, the ship slowed perceptibly. The deck was filled with Swedish sailors in merchant marine uniforms. Blond-haired sailors stood bareheaded and bowed around the uptilted canvas-covered and flag-draped body. The captain, a handsome man with thick gray hair, read the service in Swedish. From above, the piercing notes of a cornet sounded the Swedish national anthem. When the anthem was done, the strap holding the canvas-wrapped body bag was unloosed, and the weighted body shot down into the ocean. In an instant, it was lost to view. The service was done, and the ship surged forward mightily to regain its lost speed.

Mid Atlantic

The passengers (there are only ten from a handful of countries) have dinner every night at the captain's table. These are not formal occasions weighted down with proprieties. Several conversations go on at the same time. But when the captain talks of his Swedish homeland, the German occupation, and the flight of freighters to England, everybody listens. The captain is a man who has spent most of his life at sea. He has a rich sense of humor and a teasing nature. He bargains with me unmercifully, claiming that his ivory chess set is vastly superior to the one I bartered for in the Congo with Abdul, a wily Mohammedan trader. The captain will trade me even up across the board. But once having said no, I stubbornly reject the trade.

Off the coast of the United States

We are sailing north up the shoreline of the United States. Vigilance has been relaxed because American destroyer escorts are patrolling for German submarines.

New York Harbor

I was standing this morning at the railing on the ship's bow, waiting with others for the first glimpse of the United States.

The fog had been thick and beaded with moisture ever since we entered what are called the Narrows of New York Harbor. The others were wearing warm clothes, the crew was dressed in stocking caps and pea jackets, and I was wearing the khaki field jacket I wore when I paid a bitter farewell to my country so very long ago.

The fog began to dissolve into patches of cloud. Suddenly, the Statue of Liberty started to emerge over the harbor. It was green and immense. I could not hold back the tears that coursed down my cheeks.

Nor did I try.